To Tom Graziano, who substitutes a bike and the

Windy City for Huck's raft and river

—R. B.

For Sam—Huck Finn with a laptop

—B. B.

ATHENEUM BOOKS FOR YOUNG READERS
An imprint of Simon & Schuster Children's Publishing Division
1230 Avenue of the Americas, New York, New York 10020
Text copyright © 2011 by Robert Burleigh
Illustrations copyright © 2011 by Barry Blitt
ATHENEUM BOOKS FOR YOUNG READERS is a registered trademark
of Simon & Schuster, Inc.
For information about special discounts for bulk purchases, please contact Simon &
Schuster Special Sales at 1-866-506-1949 or business@simonandschuster.com.
The Simon & Schuster Speakers Bureau can bring authors to your live event. For more
information or to book an event, contact the Simon & Schuster Speakers Bureau at
1-866-248-3049 or visit our website at www.simonspeakers.com.
Book design by Debra Sfetsios and Irene Metaxatos
The text for this book is set in Bulmer MT.
The illustrations for this book are rendered in pen, ink, and watercolor.
Manufactured in China
1210 SCP
First Edition
10 9 8 7 6 5 4 3 2 1
Library of Congress Cataloging-in-Publication Data
Burleigh, Robert.
The adventures of Mark Twain by Huckleberry Finn / Robert Burleigh ; illustrated by
Barry Blitt.—1st ed.
p. cm.
ISBN 978-0-689-83041-9
1. Twain, Mark, 1835–1910—Juvenile literature. 2. Authors, American—19th century—
Biography—Juvenile literature. I. Blitt, Barry. II. Title.
PS1331.B96 2011
818'.409—dc22
[B]   2010006512

the Adventures of Mark Twain

by
Huckleberry Finn

With considerable help from Robert Burleigh and Barry Blitt

Atheneum Books for Young Readers
New York   London   Toronto   Sydney

WARNING TO THE READER

Be advised that the author of this book,

HUCKLEBERRY FINN,

is

NOT A WRITER!

In fact, he almost never went to school!

And as far as we know, he has never written another book.

MR. FINN is, well, a boy, after all.

That is why the story contains some strange ways of speaking and spelling. (It's the way many children—and grownups— spoke and spelled a long time ago in AMERICA.)

The editors of this book felt it might help readers if they were prepared for some of the special ways MR. FINN speaks.

For instance, **MR. FINN** almost always uses the word "ain't" where we say "isn't" or "is not," or "have not." Furthermore, **MR. FINN** often leaves out the letter "g" at the ends of words. For example, he says "watchin'" when he means "watching." **MR. FINN** uses old-fashioned words as well, like "I reckon" instead of "I think."

Sometimes he uses whole expressions that may make you stop and wonder. He'll say "poke your shovel into" when he means to be nosy about or interested in something. Or "there warn't much sand in his craw" when he means that someone doesn't want to do something.

BUT TRUST US. You can figure them all out, even if you have to stop here or there. And along the way, you'll get the real Mark Twain story, the story of one of America's greatest writers, as told to you by—yes!—his most famous character.

—THE EDITORS

About why I is writin' this book

ABOUT WHY I IS WRITIN' THIS BOOK

You don't know about me, without you have read a book by the name of *The Adventures of Tom Sawyer*. Or another book by the name of *Adventures of Huckleberry Finn*. Yep, you guessed it: that's me.

Now them books was writ by Mr. Mark Twain, and he told the truth, mainly. Except for a stretcher here or there. But what about Mark Twain, his own self? I ain't no highfalutin talker, but I s'pose I knowed him 'bout as well as anyone. Better 'n most, I reckon.

Didn't we float down the **same** river, layin' by and lookin' up at the sky all speckled with stars? Didn't we climb the **same** hills (tolerable long and steep they was, too), and didn't we play cops and robbers in the **same** woods? Well, thinks I, why don't *I* write down Mr. Twain's adventures, the way he writ mine? **Ain't Huck Finn got a say?**

I reckon you have seen a picture of Mark Twain. That's him over yonder when he was an **old guy,** always wearing a clean white linen suit. Which—between you and me—makes me feel gussied-up and hog-tied just to look at.

But here's somethin' you maybe ain't yet learned of: **Mark Twain warn't even his real name.** His real name was Samuel Clemens. And it's Sam I mean to fix on.

Not to worry, though. **This ain't intendin' to be some windy bioografy.** I don't lean to writin', and I don't fetch to books much neither, 'specially long ones.

But here goes.

ABOUT WHEN SAM WAS A BOY

People is always blabbin' 'bout Sam's boyhood. So I guessed I should start with that myself.

Him bein' an author, you might 'spect he went to one of them fancy-pants schools people brag about. Heck, Sam hardly went to school at all! He growed up bein' poor, same as me, in a dusty village set sideways the Mississippi River.

But bein' poor don't mean not havin' fun.

Sam was born excited. He did stuff. He tramped and skylarked and poked his shovel into whatever tripped his fancy.

He loved that big rollin' Mississippi, much as I did. He swum in it. He slung his fish bait into it. Winters, he even skated on it.

Sometimes he'd swim out to an island in the river and lay off and loaf all day, watchin' the big steamboats come chuggin' and goin', playin' hooky, free from school miserableness. (Truth is, Sam unliked school 'bout as much as I did.)

Sometimes him and his pals clumb up to a big cave near the town. They'd powwow about being outlaws, like Robin Hood. (Sam put this into his book about me and Tom Sawyer, and it's all true—that cave was mighty dark and deep.)

Yep, they was choice times. Sam pretty much went the whole hog and did what he pleased, free as a jay and lookin' out sharp for fun. **But things was about to change.**

'Cause Sam's Pap up and died when Sam was just eleven.

ABOUT SAM THE STEAMBOAT CAPTAIN

This was a hardship on Sam, for sure. Boom times was over, and he had to quick become a man.

I disremember exactly when, but after a long spell, Sam's old love of the river came back in spades. He always had a hankerin' to run one of them big steamboats. When he was just a little older than me, he paid an old riverboat pilot to teach him the ropes.

It warn't easy neither. Steamboatin' ain't somethin' any saphead can get the hang of. The river's full of bends and snags and fast currents. Sam said the Mississippi was like a book, with a new story to tell every day.

He'd stand on the top deck, hands on the wheel, feeling like a king. And I know how he felt! Maybe in Sam's story about me I jest steered a raft. But ain't it the same at night on the river, when **everything's dark?** And logs are driftin' mournful and lonesome and lanterns are twinkling from the edges of other rafts? And shoreside towns are nothing but a shiny bed of lights?

Sam met folks 'long the way. Rich and poor, white and black. The river, you could say, was Sam's schoolhouse.

But the Civil War was coming. The river was soon **clogged** with soldiers and gunboats. And steamboat days—for Sam and everyone else—was done for.

ABOUT SAM BECOMIN' A WRITER

With war fever infectin' people far and wide, Sam tried soldierin'. But it didn't take.

There warn't much sand in his craw for killin' people. And more than that, he was very unfavorable to bein' killed hisself. So he up and quit after two weeks.

Then some old cowpoke discovered silver in the hills of Nevada. Sam heard the call and wanted to waltz in on it. So he lit out and staked a claim and started hammerin' rock. But that didn't earn him no more than blisters and a sore back.

By and by Sam became a newspaper reporter. And a right good one too. When the news was thick, he writ it. And when there warn't any news, well, Sam told some real stretchers!

led, he never frowned

The feller took the money and starte...

But he was lucky, uncommon lucky

One time he called a gunslinger a name and got hisself challenged to a duel, which from he had to **skedaddle** pretty lively out of town to save his skin.

But them stretchers and stories were slowly making Sam into an **honest-to-goodness writer.** Sam's first famous story was about a gambler who bets on a jumping frog—and gets tricked and loses. The story's called *The Celebrated Jumping Frog of Calaveras County.* It's funny, and it slides down pie-easy.

Soon, book-folks said Sam was a for-real writer. That's when he tried out a new name. It was an old riverboat term he liked the gush of.

On the river, folks'd let down a rope or chain to test the depth of the water, like droppin' a stone or somethin' in a hole in the ground, to see how deep it was. **"Mark Twain"** they'd call out when the river was deep enough for the boat to pass. Sam liked the sound of it, and took it for his own.

And it stuck right nicely, too.

MARK TWAIN!

ABOUT SAM BEIN' A STAGE PERFORMER

Me, I druther wade neck-high in a hog trough than stand up before a parcel of people eyein' me up and down.

But Sam loved givin' talks to folks. He had a scratch for it—'specially when they laid out hard cash to hear him!

He read from his stories. He told about his travels. He liked to drawl and then stop in the middle of this or that, and leave the audience danglin'. Then he'd snap to—quick as a snake.

He said wise stuff like "You can't pray a lie."

He poked fun at hisself: "Nothing so needs reforming as *other people's* habits!"

And sometimes he poked fun at everyone: "There are several good protections against temptations, but the surest is cowardice!"

There's lots of sayings he says, but them's a few of my favorites.

Folks jest plain took to Sam. And it warn't long before he was givin' his talks all over the country.

ABOUT SAM'S MARRIAGE AND BIG HOUSE

Mind you, Huck Finn **ain't** sentimental. But the truth is, Sam went and fell in love. Just like that! Livy was everything Sam warn't: school-educatered, soft-talkin', and genteel.

It'd make a cow laugh to see the shines Sam started cuttin'. Soon he was trimmin' his hair, dressin' sharp, sportin' stiff shirts and silk hats, all in all what I'd call an intolerable state of discomfort. Till finally Livy said yes.

She musta' suspicioned Sam would never grow up, though, 'cause her nickname for him was "Youth"!

Sam built him and Livy a house out East, in the state of
Connecticut, near big as a steamboat. There was tons a' rooms, a
slew of baths, a marble floor, and an outside part all wedding-caked
with turrets, spires, and balconies.

On the third floor Sam snuck in a billiard room. He loved
games, 'specially billiards, which he liked to say was better for his
health than seein' doctors.

There was even a newfangled telerphone. And the food was prime. None of your low-down corn pone, but quality vittles morning, noon, and night.

(I mighta' taken to a house like that myself—for about a week or two. But then I'd hear the dogs callin' in the woods and light out again! Sam knew right well to keep me where I was—by that old river!)

They was happy here too, Sam and Livy was. They had three daughters. I reckon you could say the years swum by, they slid along so quiet and smooth and lovely.

ABOUT SAM'S BEST WELL-KNOWED BOOKS

Livy was always askin' Sam to talk about his days on the Mississippi. Maybe it was this that got his rememberies up. There's no knowin' for certain, but in the end his famousest books is about times when he was a boy.

The Adventures of Tom Sawyer (wherein I plays a very important part myself, if it don't seem like peacockin' to say so) tells about the doin's of a boy, sorta like Sam was way back. Tom gets into scrapes. But he uses his wits to unsnarl hisself.

And there ain't no hidin' the fact that
Adventures of Huckleberry Finn is most about
me and some of the troubles I got into—and about
the time Jim, a black slave, and me was raftin'
downriver, lookin' to be free.

Jim's hightailin' from bein' slaved. Me, I'm
runnin' from the Widow Douglas. She was always makin'
me to comb up on Sundays or eat food with a fork 'stead of
my fingers. (Which, seems to me, destroys the taste
considerable.)

What happens on the way—the scary stuff and the funny stuff—
I leave for you to find out!

Some folks didn't take to Sam's writin' the way real people
(like me) talks. But Sam didn't care. He writ it like he heard it.
And pretty soon, he warn't just famous. He was rich.

ABOUT SAM'S SAD LAST YEARS

It gravels me to say so, but I got to: Sam's last years was troubles.
Bad luck stuff started happenin', like what does when someone's gone
and killed a spider.

Sam gambled in the stock market and lost. He started a
book company that went bust. He sank cash into flopheaded
inventions that didn't have no more chance than a rat in a cobra cage.

At last, he was dead-for-earnest broke.

Then his favorite daughter, Susy, up and suddenly dies. Then
Livy gets sick and dies. Sam was by hisself, mostly, sort of wallowin'
around in the blackness of darkness.

But he warn't done yet.

He was now a celebrity, hullabalooed all over the world. People wrote him from everywhere. Reporters came to his house every morning. Sam would jest lie in bed and jaw away. Whatever they asked, he had answers for. And some of 'em was kinda sharp-edged, too.

Point of for instance. Sam loved America. But it scorched him seein' white folk bullyraggin' black folk 'cause their skin color was different. And he said so out loud.

(Course me and Sam thinks kind of alike in this matter. That's why I decided to help Jim escape on the raft, ain't it?)

And Sam didn't take much to some of them politicians. "When you are in politics," he says once, "you are in a wasp's nest with a short shirt-tail."

"When in doubt," Sam liked to say, "tell the truth."

Which is advice I most highly recommendate.

The year Sam was borned, Halley's Comet passed over the Earth. Sam always identified hisself with that comet, which flashes across the sky and disappears every seventy-five years.

So just before it come 'round again, seventy-five years later, Sam up and tells folks: **"It will be the greatest disappointment of my life, if I don't go out with Halley's Comet."**

And right sure enough—
he did.

LAST WORDS, 'CAUSE EVERY STORY MUST GOT SOME

Well, I done it.

I left a lot out, too, which is fer you to fill in later.

I coulda throwed more style into it, but I can't do that very handy, not being brung up to it.

I got Sam to thank for being purty well-knowed myself. Before I came along, most folks wouldn't pay no attention to a story 'bout a no-account boy gettin' into scrapes all the time. And they wouldn't like that my words ain't always presented in the King's English. But to Sam, I was just as interestin' as any of them royal mucky-mucks.

Still, bein' a character in a book ain't all peaches an' cream. 'Cause a character's got to go through the same stuff **again and again and again.** Till he's near bored to death!

Maybe school-folks who study Sam will say I'm pokin' my shovel into somethin' that ain't my business.

But, says I, Sam's adventures and Sam's stories is for everyone. Period.

And I'll jest leaf it at that.

Yours truly,

HUCKLEBERRY FINN

EDITOR'S NOTE

Since Mr. Finn's manuscript contains no dates and leaves out some important details, the editors have decided to add the material below, related to the life of Mark Twain (a.k.a. Samuel Clemens).

NOVEMBER 30, 1835
Samuel Langhorne Clemens is born in Florida, Missouri.

1839-1853
Sam Clemens grows up in Hannibal, Missouri. After his father dies, he goes to work learning the printing trade.

1853-1857
Clemens travels about the eastern part of the United States, working as a printer.

1857-1861
Clemens becomes a steamboat pilot, working up and down the Mississippi River.

1861-1866
Clemens briefly joins a Confederate militia. He travels to Nevada and mines for silver. He begins to work as a newspaper reporter and publishes his first famous story, *The Celebrated Jumping Frog of Calaveras County*. He starts using the pen name of Mark Twain.

1866-1869
Clemens travels to Hawaii and to Europe, writing newspaper stories about both trips. He publishes his first book, about the European trip, *The Innocents Abroad*. He also begins his career as a public speaker.

1870-1895
Clemens marries Olivia (Livy) Langdon in 1870. They build a large house in Hartford, Connecticut, and live there for many years. During this time Clemens publishes *The Adventures of Tom Sawyer*, *Adventures of Huckleberry Finn*, *Life on the Mississippi*, and other books. He also invests large amounts of money in various unsuccessful enterprises.

1896-1904
Clemens finally loses most of his money. He goes on a world tour and pays back all the money he owes. His favorite daughter, Susy, dies in 1896. Livy dies in 1904.

1904-1910
Clemens is now recognized as one of the most famous writers in the world. He continues to write stories and essays, even though his subjects become less joyful.

APRIL 21, 1910
Samuel Clemens (Mark Twain) dies in Redding, Connecticut, at the age of seventy-five.

MISSISSIPPI

BY MARK TWAIN